better together*

*This book is best read together, grownup and kid.

a
kids
book
about

a
kids
book
about

BEING

NONBINARY

by Hunter Chinn-Raicht

in partnership with *The GenderCool Project*

A Kids Co.
Editor Denise Morales Soto
Designers Rick DeLucco & Duke Stebbins
Creative Director Rick DeLucco
Studio Manager Kenya Feldes
Sales Director Melanie Wilkins
Head of Books Jennifer Goldstein
CEO and Founder Jelani Memory

DK
Editor Emma Roberts
Senior Production Editor Jennifer Murray
Senior Production Controller Louise Minihane
Senior Acquisitions Editor Katy Flint
Acquisitions Project Editor Sara Forster
Managing Art Editor Vicky Short
Publishing Director Mark Searle
DK would like to thank Jamie Windust

This American Edition, 2024
Published in the United States by DK Publishing
1745 Broadway, 20th Floor, New York, NY 10019

A catalog record for this book is available from the Library of Congress.
ISBN: 978-0-7440-9471-8

DK books are available at special discounts when purchased in bulk for
sales promotions, premiums, fund-raising, or educational use. For details, contact:
DK Publishing Special Markets, 1745 Broadway, 20th Floor, New York, NY 10019, or SpecialSales@dk.com

Printed and bound in China

www.dk.com

akidsco.com

This book was made with Forest
Stewardship Council™ certified
paper – one small step in DK's
commitment to a sustainable future.
For more information go to
www.dk.com/our-green-pledge

To every kiddo out there who is living
the life they were always meant to live,
and to the grownups who believe in them.

To all our GenderCool Champion friends
whose voices helped make this book a reality.
We are changing the world: Alex, Ashton,
Chazzie, Daniel, Eve, Gia, Greyson,
Jonathan, Kai, Landon, Lia, Max,
Rebekah, Rose, Sivan, Stella, and Tru.

Intro
for grownups

In 2019, the *Merriam-Webster Dictionary* named the word "they" Word of the Year. Of the thousands of words in the English language, these folks put a common pronoun on a pedestal. Why do you think that is? Well, because there's nothing common about the word "they." The word has expanded and is now used by some nonbinary people to help express who they are to others. Nonbinary people may choose to use any combination of pronouns—they/them, he/they, and she/they are just a few examples.

Most people tell us they don't understand what nonbinary means, but the interest in learning is huge! That's where Hunter and this book come in—to introduce you to what it means to be nonbinary.

But keep in mind that there's no 1 way to be nonbinary. For some, their personal sense of self doesn't fit the binary way that most people look at gender. For others, it's more than 1 gender or feeling no strong connection to any gender. There are as many ways to be nonbinary as there are people! This book is here to help open the door to understanding.

—The GenderCool Team

Hi, my name is **Hunter**,
and my pronouns
are they/them.

I'm nonbinary
and I'm a dancer.

I've been performing on stage most of my life, and I love to dance anywhere I can, even alone in my bedroom!

It's one of my favorite
things to do, actually.

Did you know that sometimes
when dancers perform,
they dance in pairs?

When this happens,
typically a boy is
partnered with a girl.

Because I'm nonbinary,
I can dance either
partner's role.

Have you ever heard the word **NON-BINARY?**

Do you know what it means?

If you don't, that's **OK**!
That's why I'm here!

The word **nonbinary**
can mean a lot of different
things to different people.

And really, to talk about being nonbinary, we also need to talk about what **binary** means.

Binary is a fancy way to say made up of 2 directly opposite things.

When we talk about the gender binary, it means being a **boy** or a **girl**.

When you are born, the doctor who delivers you says, **"It's a boy!"** or, **"It's a girl!"** based on your body.

BUT GENDER ISN'T THAT SIMPLE.

To me, gender is a big, beautiful word with room for all of us.
It means a lot of different things to different people, but this is what I want you to know first...

Gender is how you feel in your heart and mind, but it may not match what the doctor says when you are born.

For me, to be nonbinary means I am not a girl or a boy; I am somewhere outside of that.

I've always loved exploring things like trying new hairstyles and wearing lots of different outfits every day.

It makes me smile when I go to bed as a human every night.

When I was growing up,
I would always take a couple
of different outfits to
school with me.

I would go to school wearing something pink, or a dress I found hanging in my closet. A dress and the colour pink are usually considered to be more feminine.*

Feminine is how we describe something that is typically associated with girls. However, this doesn't mean that everything that is feminine is for girls—it's for everyone!

Then, as the day went on, wearing these clothes wouldn't feel right or comfortable anymore. So I would happily switch to the more traditionally masculine* clothes that I kept in my locker.

***Masculine** is how we describe something that is typically associated with boys, but people of all genders can like things that are masculine.

This usually meant some gym shorts and a jersey, or my favorite button-up tuxedo shirt.

Over time, this became a way for me to express who I am, in my own unique way that's just right for me. I am outside of the pink and blue stereotype.*

*__*The pink and blue stereotype*__ is that pink is a color only for girls and blue is a color only for boys. It's like dresses being only for girls or tuxedo shirts only for boys.*

I am
gray,
white,
and

ALL THE

COLORS

mashed up into one!

Nonbinary means
something different
to everyone!

It never looks
or feels the same
from 1 person
to the next.

Being nonbinary may seem like I'm trying to fit in a different box.

Instead, it's about feeling a freedom that comes with not having to fit in a box that other people tell me I should fit into.

This may not make a lot of sense, but not understanding is a great place to start!

I love answering questions and having conversations about the differences in who I am compared to the gender binary.

When I told my friends and teachers at school about who I truly am, they didn't mind!

They were

HAPPY FOR ME!

But often, I have to explain and define new words for them.

They made a lot of mistakes,
but they handled them
and didn't stop trying.
It made me so proud.

It takes a lot of courage
to mess up and
keep trying!

If someone slips up, the best thing for them to do is briefly apologize, correct themselves, and move on.

For example:

"SORRY, I MEANT THEY."

Then keep going with whatever you were talking about.

Trying is the most important part.

It makes all the difference.

Like my Spanish teacher,
for example.

In the Spanish language,
all words are assigned
a gender.

People, places, and even things.

Like "la lámpara"—the lamp.

The "la" in "la lámpara"
tells us that it's supposed to
be feminine.

Same thing with
"el vaso"—the cup.

The "el" tells us that it's
supposed to be masculine.

Interesting, right?

There aren't a lot of gender-neutral* words in Spanish, so it was difficult for me to find ways to express myself.

Gender neutral is a way to describe words that don't have a specific binary gender.

Luckily, my Spanish
teacher taught me
how to use new words
that describe me,

**without being so
pink and blue.**

So, instead of saying something like, "Ladies and gentlemen," to get everyone's attention, my teacher would say,

"HEY, EVERYONE!"

If more people use gender-neutral words in their day-to-day life, we can start to reverse the idea that everything needs to be feminine or masculine.

Words are important.

They help us understand
each other, right?

And more importantly,
they can help us
understand ourselves.

Having the words to describe yourself can feel so great, but there doesn't have to be a word for who you are.

And that's OK!

That can feel great too!

Maybe nonbinary describes exactly who you are.

Maybe it doesn't.

Whether there is a word which fits you or not, your experience is true to one person—you!

GENUINE.

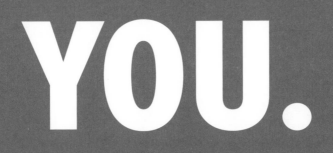

Even if it's outside the
gender binary.

This is **your** dance, after all.

Outro
for grownups

Now that you've read this book, you and the kid in your life are likely processing all sorts of things. That's OK! It'll take some time for it all to sink in. The good news is, there are societies all over the world who've traveled this path before us. We can learn from them!

On nearly every continent and for all of recorded history, thriving cultures have recognized, revered, and integrated more than 2 genders. Many societies in the US have long-established traditions regarding multiple genders. For example, there is a native Hawaiian culture whose tradition is to revere people who embody both male and female spirit and are known as māhū.

With this new understanding, get out there with your kid and meet more people! Seek out those who are different from you. And when you meet a nonbinary person (and you will), welcome them into your world with a smile and with respect. They are amazing people!

—The GenderCool Team

About The Author

Hunter Chinn-Raicht (they/them) is an aerial acrobat, animal shelter volunteer, identifies as nonbinary, and can't open envelopes without completely tearing them apart. They hope for the day when all genders are celebrated.

Their voice helps fuel The GenderCool Project, a youth-led movement replacing misinformed opinions with positive experiences meeting transgender and nonbinary youth who are thriving. Through education, advocacy, leadership development, and visibility, GenderCool is uniquely impacting culture, policy, and business worldwide. Learn more at GenderCool.org

 @gendercool   @gendercool   🌐 www.gendercool.org

Made to empower.

a kids book about **racism**
by Jelani Memory

a kids book about ANXIETY
by Ross Szabo

a kids book about DISABILITY
by Kristine Napper

a kids book about IMAGINATION
by LEVAR BURTON

a kids book about *belonging*
by Kevin Carroll

a kids book about **failyure**
by Dr. Laymon Hicks

a kids book about GRATITUDE
by Ben Kenyon

a kids book about LIFE ONLINE
by Dave S. Anderson & Blake Fleischacker

a kids book about *body image*
by Rebecca Alexander

a kids book about IMMIGRATION
by MJ Calderon

a kids book about EMPATHY
by Daron K. Roberts

a kids book about GENDER
by Dale Mueller

a kids book about Love
by ZIGGY MARLEY

a kids book about EQUALITY
by BILLIE JEAN KING

a kids book about MONEY
by Adam Stramwasser

a kids book about FEMINISM
by Emma McIlroy

a kids book about *adventure*
by Dr. Ben Tertin

a kids book about CLIMATE CHANGE
by Zanagee Artis & Olivia Greenspan

a kids book about CONFIDENCE
by Joy Cho

a kids book about BEING NONBINARY
by Hunter Chinn-Raicht
in partnership with The GenderCool Project

Discover more at akidsco.com